I0560651

Jesus became poor for **Michelle's** sake so that through His poverty **she** might become rich in every way.

— 2 Corinthians 8:9

Michelle's Finances and Prosperity

SCRIPTURE DECLARATIONS

Personalized Scriptures
to Speak Provision &
Increase in Your Life

MyVersion LLC.

Michelle's Finances and Prosperity Scripture Declarations
Personalized Scriptures to Speak Provision & Increase in Your Life

Print Edition
ISBN 13: 979-8-89846-002-0
Copyright © 2025 MyVersion LLC.

All Scripture quotations in this book are carefully adapted from public domain translations such as the King James Version (KJV). Some verses have been slightly modified to reflect the reader's name and to adjust for tense, voice, or clarity, In all cases, great care has been taken to preserve the original meaning and context of the passage.

Published by MyVersion LLC.
https://MyVersionBook.com

Contents

Introduction

Abundance for His Children

God has always delighted in providing abundantly for His children. From the very beginning, Scripture shows us that lack was never part of His design—He desires to bless us, meet our every need, and equip us to fulfill the calling He's placed on our lives.

Whether you're seeking wisdom for debt reduction, the resources to start a new venture, or a greater ability to give generously, this book will guide you to discover and declare God's promises over your finances.

These financial confessions are more than positive words; they are rooted in the life-changing truth of God's Word. The Bible teaches that we activate faith by speaking and hearing what God has already declared (Romans 10:17). As you align your speech with His Word, you'll find fresh faith rising in your heart and practical answers for your everyday life.

No matter your current financial situation, the promises in both the Old and New Testaments demonstrate that God is your Provider, your Source, and your Sustainer.

As you read through this book, take ownership of each verse and speak it out loud over your life. Whether it's for daily provision, debt freedom, or the resources to accomplish your God-given assignment, let these confessions stir up faith in your heart. Expect to see big changes in your finances and in every realm of your life as you agree with God's promises and put His Word into action.

Michelle's

Provision

Promises

from the

Old Covenant

God is making **Michelle** into a great nation. He blesses **Michelle**, makes **her** name great, and causes **her** to be a blessing to others.

- Genesis 12:2

Michelle walks in covenant with God, so **she** is abundantly blessed in every resource He provides.

- Genesis 13:2

Everything **Michelle** does prospers because the Lord is with **her**. He causes all that **she** does to succeed.

- Genesis 39:3

The Lord rains bread from heaven for **Michelle**; and **she** is able to eat and be full every day.

- Exodus 16:4

Michelle remembers the Lord **her** God: He gives **her** the power to gain wealth and confirms the covenant He has with **her** today.

- Deuteronomy 8:18

Michelle is blessed when **she** comes in, and **she** is blessed when **she** goes out. The Lord commands His blessing on **her** storehouses and everything **she** sets **her** hand to. **Michelle** is blessed in the land the Lord has given **her**.

- Deuteronomy 28:6, 8

God grants **Michelle** abundant prosperity. He blesses the fruit of **her** body, **her** resources, and **her** livelihood. The Lord gives **her** access to His good treasure and blesses the work of **her** hands. **She** will lend to many nations and not borrow.

- Deuteronomy 28:11-12

Michelle keeps God's covenant and follows His Word; therefore, **she** prospers in everything **she** does.

- *Deuteronomy* 29:9

The Lord causes **Michelle** to abound in everything **she** puts **her** hands to; in the fruit of **her** body, in the fruit of **her** resources, and in the fruit of **her** land, all for **her** good: for the LORD rejoices over **Michelle** for good!

- *Deuteronomy* 30:9

The Word of God does not depart from **Michelle's** mouth; **she** meditates on it day and night and obeys it. Because of that, **her** way is prosperous, and **she** has good success. — *Joshua* 1:8

Riches and honor come from God. He empowers **Michelle**, strengthens **her**, and makes **her** great.

— *1 Chronicles* 29:12

Michelle delights in God's Word and refuses ungodly counsel. **She** is like a fruitful tree planted by the water; everything **she** does prospers.

— *Psalm* 1:1-3

The Lord is **Michelle's** Shepherd; **she** shall not want. **She** has all that **she** needs.

He anoints **Michelle's** head with oil and **her** cup runs over!

Goodness and mercy follow **her** all the days of **her** life.

- Psalm 23:1,5,6

Michelle does not lack or suffer hunger. Because **she** seeks the Lord, **she** has everything **she** needs.

- Psalm 34:10

God delights in **Michelle's** prosperity. **She** rejoices in His goodness and says continually, "The Lord be magnified!"

- Psalm 35:27

Michelle has never been forsaken by God and **her** children will never beg for bread. God is merciful and gives generously. **Michelle** is His seed, and **she** is blessed!

- Psalm 37:25-26

Blessed be the Lord who saved **Michelle**, He loads **her** with benefits each and every day.

- Psalm 68:19

God alone is **Michelle's** judge and promoter. He lifts **her** up to the position He has prepared for **her**.

- Psalm 75:7

The Lord is **Michelle's** sun and shield; He grants **her** grace and glory, withholding no good thing from **her**.

- Psalm 84:11

Wealth and riches are in **Michelle's** house. The goodness of God endures forever.

- Psalm 112:3

The Lord increases **Michelle** more and more—**her** and **her** family. **She** is blessed by the Lord who created the heavens and earth!

- Psalm 115:14-15

Michelle trusts in the Lord above all else. **Her** confidence rests in Him, not in other people, leaders, or government officials.

- Psalm 118:8-9

Michelle does not place **her** trust in human strength or government, for true help comes from the Lord.

- Psalm 146:3

Because **Michelle** honors the Lord with **her** wealth and the first-fruits of all **her** increase; **her** barns are filled and overflow, and **her** vats are brimming over with new wine!

- Proverbs 3:9-10

Michelle works diligently, and that diligence brings **her** to abundance.

- Proverbs 10:4

The blessing of the Lord makes **Michelle** rich, and He adds no sorrow [painful toil] with it.

- Proverbs 10:22

Michelle gives generously and sees increase; **she** refuses to withhold what God leads **her** to sow.

- Proverbs 11:24

Michelle gathers wealth steadily and honestly, and **her** resources increase.

- Proverbs 13:11

Michelle leaves an inheritance for **her** children's children, and the wealth of the sinner is stored up for **Michelle.**

- Proverbs 13:22

All **Michelle's** labor yields profit. **She** acts on **her** ideas rather than just talking about them.

- Proverbs 14:23

When **Michelle** gives to the poor, **she** is lending to the Lord Himself, and He repays **her** with His abundant provision.

- Proverbs 19:17

Michelle avoids unwise debt, staying free so that **she** is never ruled by lenders.

- Proverbs 22:7

Michelle shares with the poor and will never be in lack, for the Lord sees **her** generosity and blesses **her** in return.

- Proverbs 28:27

Michelle is willing and obedient, so **she** can eat the good of the land.

- Isaiah 1:19

Michelle brings **her** tithes to God's storehouse, and He opens the windows of heaven, pouring **her** out a blessing too big to contain.

All nations call **her** blessed. God brings **her** into a fruitful and delightful land.

- Malachi 3:10,12

Michelle's Financial Realities in the New Covenant

Michelle gives in secret, and **her** heavenly Father rewards **her** openly. *- Matthew* 6:4

Michelle serves God—not money. Money serves **her** as **she** follows God's will. **Michelle** does not worry because the Lord takes care of **her** clothes, food, and all **her** necessities.

- Matthew 6:24-26

Michelle seeks first the Kingdom of God and His righteousness, and all the things **she** need are added to **her**. *- Matthew* 6:33

If **Michelle** will say to a mountain, "Be removed, and be cast into the sea;" and does not doubt in **her** heart, but believes what **she** says will come to pass; **she** will have whatever **she** says.

- *Mark* 11:23-24

Michelle gives, and it is given back to **her**; good measure, pressed down, shaken together, and running over, others give back to **her**. As **she** sows generously, it will be given back to **her** in abundance and generously.

- *Luke* 6:38

Michelle uses **her** resources wisely for eternal impact. **She** is faithful with little and because of that, **she** is entrusted with much and true riches.

- Luke 16:9-11

The enemy came to steal, to kill, and to destroy. Jesus came so **Michelle** could have life, and have it more abundantly.

- John 10:10

Michelle works diligently and is able to support the weak, remembering that it is more blessed to give than to receive.

- Acts 20:35

If God did not spare His own Son but gave Him for **Michelle**, then **she** should trust Him to freely give **her** all good things.

- Romans 8:3

Jesus became poor for **Michelle's** sake so that through His poverty **Michelle** might become rich in every way.

- 2 Corinthians 8:9

Michelle sows generously and reaps generously. **She** is a cheerful giver, and God loves that **she** gives freely.

- 2 Corinthians 9:6-7

God makes all grace abound toward **Michelle**, so **she** has all sufficiency in every area and an abundance for every good work.

- 2 Corinthians 9:8

God provides seed for **Michelle** to sow and bread for **her** to eat. He multiplies it, increasing the harvest of **her** righteousness.

Michelle is enriched in all things and in every way so **she** can be generous and **her** generosity can point people back to God in thanksgiving!

- 2 Corinthians 9:10-11

Michelle's God supplies all **her** needs according to His riches in glory by Christ Jesus.

- Philippians 4:19

Michelle refuses to trust in uncertain riches. Instead, **she** trusts in the living God who richly gives **her** all things to enjoy.

- 1 Timothy 6:17

Michelle prospers and enjoys good health even as **her** soul prospers.

- 3 John 1:2

Prayer For Finances & Prosperity

Heavenly Father, in the mighty name of Jesus, I come before You with confidence and boldness, knowing that You are my Source and Provider (Philippians 4:19). Your Word declares that You give me power to get wealth so You can establish Your covenant in my life (Deuteronomy 8:18), and I receive that power right now by faith. I thank You that the blessing of the Lord makes me rich, and You add no sorrow with it (Proverbs 10:22).

Lord, I stand on Your promises, declaring that wealth and riches are in my house, and that my righteousness endures forever (Psalm 112:3). Just as You daily load me with benefits (Psalm 68:19), I expect to see Your supernatural provision manifest in every area of my finances. I sow generously into Your kingdom, trusting that I will also reap generously (2 Corinthians 9:6), and I believe You multiply the seed I sow and increase the fruits of my righteousness (2 Corinthians 9:10).

I speak to every mountain of lack and debt, commanding it to be removed and cast into the sea (Mark 11:23). I call forth new opportunities, divine connections, and creative ideas for prosperity. I decree that I have the mind of Christ (1 Corinthians 2:16) and walk in wisdom to steward the resources You've entrusted to me. Thank You, Father, that You supply all my needs according to Your riches in glory by Christ Jesus (Philippians 4:19). I rejoice that You are my Good Shepherd; I shall not want (Psalm 23:1). In Jesus' name, I pray and believe—Amen

PRAYER FOR SALVATION AND BAPTISM IN THE HOLY SPIRIT

Heavenly Father, I come to You now in the Name of Jesus. Your Word says that, "Whosoever shall call on the name of the Lord shall be saved" (Acts 2:21 KJV). I am calling on You. I pray and confess Jesus as Lord over my life according to Romans 10:9-10 (KJV): "If thou shalt confess with thy mouth the Lord Jesus, and shalt believe in thine heart that God hath raised him from the dead, thou shalt be saved. For with the heart man believeth unto righteousness; and with the mouth confession is made unto salvation." I do that now. I confess that Jesus is Lord, and I believe in my heart that God raised Him from the dead.

I am now reborn! I am a Christian—a child of Almighty God! I am saved!

You also said in your Word, "If ye then, being evil know how to give good gifts unto your children: HOW MUCH MORE shall your heavenly Father give the Holy Spirit to them that ask him?" (Luke 11:13 KJV). I'm asking now... fill me with your Holy Spirit. Holy Spirit, rise up within me as I praise God. I fully expect to speak with other tongues as you give me the utterance (Acts 2:4). In Jesus Name, Amen!

Begin to praise God for filling you with the Holy Spirit. Speak those words and syllables you receive—not in your own language, but the language given to you by the Holy Spirit. You have to use your own voice. God will not force you to speak. Don't be concerned with how it sounds. It is a heavenly language!

Praise God, Michelle! You are a healed, born-again, Spirit-filled believer. You'll never be the same again. Find a good church that boldly preaches God's Word and obeys it. Become part of a church family who will love and care for you as you love and care for them.

MyVersion LLC.

We hope you enjoyed this personalized declarations book. Looking for more topics like healing, peace, or your identity in Christ? MyVersion Publishing offers books just like this in nearly 100 popular male and female names as well as in personalized "I am" confessions.

You can find your name or your friend's name on Amazon.com or on our website at MyVersionBook.com, these mini-books are a convenient 4x6 inch pocket sized paperback, ebook, audiobook, or Kindle;

perfect for gift-giving or keeping in your pocket as a source of encouragement wherever you go.

Visit our website now to get your personalized books!